EQUIPPING CHILDREN
THROUGH   PRAYER

787
Generation

EQUIPPING CHILDREN THROUGH PRAYER

A MANUAL FOR TRAINING CHILDREN TO HEAR THE VOICE OF GOD

PURPOSE

PRAYING LIKE JESUS PRAYED

1- To equip the Smaller Saints to hear the Voice of God by using the Apostolic Prayers to pray for their families, church, city, schools, the nations.

2- To help children learn how to enjoy prayer and have a relationship with the Father, by using The Word of God.

3- To be a tool to train other leaders in equipping children and youth to pray the Word.

4 - To be a simple tool so anyone can teach children to pray like Jesus Prayed, using the Word of God.

Making Disciples of Children Through Prayer is a publication of Writeitplain Publishing and The

787 Generation. You can find more information on the 787 Generation at 787Generation.com.

We are committed to disciple, train, and equip a generation. Our mission is based on Psalm

78:6-8.

787generation@gmail.com is the contact for Joseph Floyd and

Darlene Floyd.

Blessings

DEDICATION

Joey and I would like to dedicate this manual to

God, who taught us through his Son, Jesus, and

the Holy Spirit, how to pray.

Also, this manual is dedicated to Tracy and Lenny

LaGuardia, who taught us everything we know about

Children's Ministry.

WHAT GLORY IS THERE IN CHILDREN'S MINISTRY?

Why are we here? What is on The Father's heart?

Our story: It's all about the Father's Heart. I (Joey) had no desire to be in Children's ministry, but God used a two-year-old to teach me Apostolic prayers. Apostolic prayers are the prayers that the Apostles, for example, Paul, Peter, John, and Jesus, prayed in the Bible.

We believe there is a revival coming through the children and youth. Therefore, we must prepare for His return. Part of that mandate is to train and disciple children and youth to live ready for Christ's return.

These lessons will prepare children and youth through the Bible and prayer for more than revival. They will help prepare for life as disciples of Christ.

These lessons cover intimacy with Jesus, prayer, and worship. The lessons in the other books in this series will cover God's Heart For The Nations, Israel and the Abrahamic Blessings, The Armor of God, and The Beatitudes. Also, there will be a book dedicated to the Tabernacle, worship, the priests, and furnishings, demonstrating how Christ fulfilled them all.

The children's one-hour Call to the Wall meeting has a lesson, craft, and snack. Snacks can be given while the class is taught, as that works best for the sake of time. After snack, lesson, craft time, and a lesson review, we go to a time for Worship and Prayer.

Why We Are Here Continued

We focus on learning the Apostolic Prayers with motions during Prayer time. You can find the motions to the Apostolic Prayers on Youtube under David Harder at the following links:

https://www.youtube.com/watch?v=06i6QgUfY5Q.

https://www.youtube.com/watch?v=QHRE1SMhqig

https://www.youtube.com/watch?v=2mqxFYcUqKA

Sometimes, the Holy Spirit leads us into "Prayer Cave Time," allowing children to enjoy quiet worship and prayer led by the Holy Spirit.

Children's workers: Always pray and be led by the Holy Spirit because no Call to the Wall will be the same. We want the Holy Spirit to be in control of every lesson.

Blessings,

Joey and Darlene

Mission, Vision, And Goals For Children's Call To Prayer

Mission: To prepare and equip a generation to know God and His Son, Jesus Christ, through worship, prayer, the word, and serving. To train and prepare a generation to walk with the Spirit of God, keep His commandments, and do His works.

Vision: To see a generation raised living wholeheartedly for Jesus and prepared for His return!

Goal: 1) To establish prayer, worship, and the word as priorities in the lives of a rising generation so that they will live devoted lives in the kingdom, fascinated with God and His Son. 2) To equip a generation to understand God's call and heart for Israel and the nations.

Scripture Mandate for 787 Generation: Psalm 78:4-8 (NASB)

4-We will not conceal them from their children But tell to the generation to come the praises of the Lord, And His strength, and His wondrous works that He has done.

5- For He established a testimony in Jacob and appointed a law in Israel, which He commanded our fathers That they should teach them to their children,

6- That the generation to come might know, even the children yet to be born, that they may arise and tell them to their children,

7- That they should put their confidence in God and not forget the works of God, But comply with His commandments,

Mission, Vision Goals Continued

8- and not be like their fathers, a stubborn and rebellious generation, a generation that did not prepare its heart and whose spirit was not faithful to God.

We must teach, train, and prepare the rising generation in the ways of the Lord. We are chosen vessels from Jesus to 'feed His lambs. This is not an hour to play games but to teach them to pray, worship, and enjoy prayer. History is full of revivals and moves of God that were soon forgotten because 'fathers and mothers' failed to fulfill Moses' words to the leaders to teach the rising generation.

Guide For Prayer Time

I. God wants everyone to pray for others.

    A. Praying for our parents,

    B. Praying for our friends

    C. Praying for Missionaries & The Nations

II. When we pray, good things will happen.

    A. We can have peace with God.

    B. God will help us make Godly choices.

    C. We have the authority to stop the Devil. Unfortunately, some prefer Satan or the 'enemy.'

III. When we pray, it draws us closer to God and builds our faith.

    A. We learn to love one another.

    B. We learn to hear God's voice.

    C. We see our prayers answered.

Note On The Table Of Contents

We have organized the Table of Contents to help you quickly find the lessons and corresponding Apostolic Prayer. Following each lesson will be the craft instruction pages, and following the instruction pages will be a coloring page or similar craft page in many cases.

Thus, we have provided as much as possible to make it easier for you, the teacher, to have everything at your fingertips. You only need to add materials such as scissors, glue, construction paper, and much love. Blessings.

Table of Contents

Introductory

Lessons

For

Equipping

The 787 Generation

Introductory Lessons On Prayer

1- Jesus Teaches Us How To Pray:

Luke 11:1-11, Matthew 6:5-15

2- The Goal of Prayer:

Luke 18:1-18; Genesis 18:16-33; John 17:1-16;

Matt. 26:36-46

3- Where Two Or More Are Gathered:

Matthew 18:18-20; Acts 12:1-19

4- Confidence In prayer:

Matthew 14:13-21

5- When We Don't Pray:

Daniel 4:19-37; 2 Chronicles 7:14

Lesson: Jesus Teaches Us How To Pray
Luke 11:1-11, Matthew 6:5-15

Lesson: Jesus used an example of how to talk to God through prayer. Jesus had an

intimate relationship with God the Father. It is like having a relationship with our earthly

fathers.

When you pray, you will receive God's strength and power to help you with your

relationship with God the Good Father.

To have a relationship with a person, you will want to spend time with the person.

The disciples wanted to learn how to pray, so they asked, "Lord, teach us to pray just

as John taught his disciples."

He said, "When you pray, don't be like the hypocrites." "They love to pray to be noticed

by people, and that is the only reward that they will receive." "But, when you pray, Go to

your room, shut the door, and pray to God the Father in that secret place. Your Father

who sees you do it secretly will reward you."

The Lord's Prayer Is an example of how to pray: Matthew 6:9-14 NIV.

Jesus Teaches Us To Pray Continued

"This then is how you should pray: "Our Father in heaven, hallowed be thy name, your kingdom come, your will be done, on earth as it is in heaven. Give us today our daily bread. And forgive us our debts as we also have forgiven our debtors. And lead us not into temptation, but deliver us from the evil one." Amen

Recite this verse, and then have the students recite it with you.

Craft: Praying Hands

Snack:

Activity: Pray over a map or family/community poster.

Pray for God's kingdom to come into our family, church, city, and nation.

Craft: Jesus Teaches Us How To Pray

Supplies:

White construction paper

Crayons

Directions:

1. Before class, have the teacher write "Praying Hands" on the top of the paper.

2. Have each child trace their hands on the paper with the teacher's help.

3. Have each child color their hands.

   Explain to the children that they can hold their hands and pray the Lord's Prayer to the Father God.

Lesson: The Goal Of Prayer:

Luke 18:1-18; Genesis 18:16-33; John 17:1-16;
Matt. 26:36-46

Prayer is not based on getting what we want; it is not a wish list.

Prayer is our way of talking to God. It is like picking up your phone and talking to a friend, your mom, or your dad.

Goals: 1- Pray what is On God's heart.

2- Pray about God's purpose or calling.

3- Pray for all people to be saved and have Jesus in their hearts.

4- Pray for family, friends, and the nations.

5- Pray for Israel to receive salvation.

Even when He was dying, Jesus' goal of prayer was to surrender to God's will and not His will.

On the cross, He prayed, "Father forgive them, they know not what they do," and His last prayer was, "Father, into your hands I entrust my life." Then He died. Even in the garden, He prayed He would not have to go to the cross. In the end, He surrendered to God's will.

Jesus trusted His life to God the Father. He died but was raised from the dead and now sits at the Father's right hand.

The Goal Of Prayer Continued

When we pray according to God's will, He provides what we need, and things go much

better than when we pray for what we want.

Craft: Making a Prayer Journal

Snack:

Activity: Pray over the map and family/community poster.

Craft: The Goal Of Prayer
Craft: MY PRAYER JOURNAL

Supplies:

- 8 X 10 Colored Paper (Or Construction Paper)

- White Prayer List

- Glue

- Stickers

Directions:

Step 1:

- See a sample of the craft on the following page

- Before class, fold a colored paper in half

   for each child.

- On the front page, write "MY PRAYER JOURNAL."

Step 2:

- Inside pages of the Prayer Journal

- Before class, write on the left side- Isaiah 42:8

   "I am the Lord: that is my name."

- On the right side, at the top, write the words,

   "Names of the people who need prayer."

The Goal Of Prayer Craft Continued

Step 3:

- Give each child a white prayer list.

- Have each child glue the Prayer List on the right side.

- Give each child stickers to decorate their Prayer

Journals.

Five Steps For The Goal Of Prayer
(Guide For Helping Children To Pray)

1. Pray What Is On God's Heart

2. Pray About God's Purpose And Calling For My Life

3. Pray For The Salvation Of All People: That They Would Know Jesus

4. Pray For Your Family, Friends, And People Of All Nations

5. Pray For Israel's Salvation And Pray Psalm 122:6 "Pray For The Peace Of Jerusalem; May They Be Secure Who Love You." ESV

These Steps Are A Guideline To Teach Children To Hear

God's Voice While They Are Learning How To Pray.

Make A Copy For Each Child To Take Home.

We Encourage Journaling among Children. Journaling Helps

Document Each Child's Prayer Needs, Requests, Praise,

Thanksgiving, and Dreams.

We Offer Two Journals For Children To Journal Their Prayers and

Dreams. Both are available On Amazon.

Kids Praise And Prayer Journal: I Can Talk To God

Kids Prayer And Dream Journal: I Can Hear From God

Here's the link if you would

To order a copy: https://www.amazon.com/dp/B09Q8WM2PV

Lesson: When Two Or More Are Gathered

Acts 12:1-19

There are times in our prayer lives when we need to come together in groups and join our hearts for one purpose----- to seek God's power, grace, faithfulness, and His will for a situation.

As in the story in Acts 12:1-19, King Herod puts Peter in prison because he would not stop telling them the 'good news' of Jesus, which made the Jews happy. Peter had 15-20 soldiers guarding him. King Herod waited until after the feast of Passover to charge Peter with crimes proclaiming Jesus as King instead of Herod or The Emperor.

While Peter was waiting in prison, the church met and prayed for Peter.

Peter was asleep, bound in chains between two soldiers, as another soldier guarded the entrance.

Suddenly, while Peter slept, an angel appeared and awakened him and told him to get his shoes on, get dressed, and follow him.

He followed the angel to the house where the church was meeting in prayer for him.

But they were afraid to open the door because they thought Herod might be coming for them. Later, Peter told them what happened after they let him in.

Imagine their surprise to find Peter was released supernaturally. That should increase our faith.

When Two Or More Are Gathered: Continued

There are times when we need each other, and prayer binds us together for a common purpose. Then we can see God do great things through prayer.

Craft: Make paper chains with the words of the Lord's Prayer

Snack:

Activity: Pray over Family and Community

Craft: Where Two Or More Are Gathered

Craft: Prayer Chains

Supplies:

- Make copies of the Lord's Prayer found in the Appendix
  for each child.
- Tape

Directions:

Step 1:

- Before class, cut paper into strips to make chains,
- On the back of the strips, number them 1 thru 6.
- Make a Prayer chain to show the children how a
  Paperchain should look.

Step 2:

- Give each child the strips of The Lord's Prayer.
  Help Instruct the children on how to make a paper chain,
- Give each child six pieces of tape and instruct them how to
  tape the chain.
- Help the children to put them in number order.
  (If it isn't in number order, it is okay, just let them
  enjoy Craft Time)

Confidence In Prayer
Matthew 14:13-21

Jesus always sought God in prayer before He did anything. When it came to the Father, Jesus wasn't shy- He came with confidence and boldness.

He believed God would answer His prayers and the Father's will would be done. Jesus believed God was always with Him.

We can have that same confidence in prayer when we seek God with a pure and clean heart, forgive others, and trust Him with our prayers to believe His will to be done.

There is a story relating to the confidence Jesus had in prayer. It is called the "Feeding of the 5,000.'

One day, Jesus got in a boat to be by Himself. The crowd of people had heard what He did. They hear about His miracles, healings, and signs and wonders. They followed Him on foot. When Jesus saw the crowd, He had compassion for the people and healed the sick.

The sun started to set, and His disciples told Jesus to send the people away because they were hungry, to at least let them go into town to find food. They were hungry, and they had no food.

Confidence In Prayer: Continued

But, Jesus told them, " there is no need for you to send them away or for you to go looking." They told Jesus all they could find in the crowd were five loaves of bread and two small fishes.

Jesus told the disciples to bring Him the food and instructed the crowd to be seated. He had confidence in His Father and took and blessed the bread and fish. Then the disciples distributed the food, and the people ate and were full.

When they finished eating, there were 12 baskets of food left over. Therefore, we must be confident God will answer our prayers when we pray according to His will.

Craft: 5 loaves and two fishes

Snack: Crackers and goldfish

Activity: Pray over the map using Apostolic Prayers
Have the children pray for families, churches, communities, the states, and the nations as they feel led. Feel free to encourage, guide, or help them if they feel stuck.

Worship and private prayer time.

Confidence In Prayer
Craft: 5 Loaves and 2 Fishes

Supplies:

- Copies of the "5 Loaves and 2 Fishes" coloring
  Page found in the Appendix.

- Scissors

- Crayons

- Paper Plates

- Glue

Directions:

Step 1:

- Give each child a copy of the coloring page, and
  Crayons.

- Give each child scissors to cut out the five loaves and
  Two fish.
  (The teacher may want to cut out the loaves and fish
  before class, if you have younger children.)

Step 2:

- Give each child a paper plate to color.
  The plate is to be their basket for the loaves and fishes.

Step 3:

- Have the children glue the loaves and fishes to the plate.

When We Don't Pray
Luke 15:11-32

What Happens when we don't pray?

When we stop praying, it blocks us from staying in God's presence. We quit talking to God, think of our desires, and when we are tempted, we fall into sin. We stop thinking about what God wants and walk away from Him and all His promises.

That reminds me of the story in Luke 15, where one young man did that. There was a rich man who had two sons. So one day, the younger son said to his father, "Give me my share of the inheritance."

The father gave the son his inheritance, and he took the money and left. After that, he didn't care about his father or older brother, just himself.

The son went far away to a land where nobody knew him! Soon he had spent all his money on fancy clothes and rich food. He had no money and took a job feeding pigs. He was starving. He got a job feeding pigs. He got so hungry he sat down and ate what the pigs ate.

One day, while feeding the pigs, he finally came to his senses. My dad has servants, and they eat better than this. I am starving and eating pig slop. They have all of the food they want to eat. I will go back home.

He went home, and his father took him back.

Focus: Don't Quit praying.

1-The son didn't care about his father - He quit talking to his father. And left His father's presence.

When We Don't Pray: Continued

2- The son became selfish and greedy.

3- He ended up in a pigpen, starving and hungry. When you walk away from God, you end up hungry and dirty.

Through God's grace and the prayers of the 'Father,' he came back home. Do not stop praying. Don't end up in a pigpen.

Craft: Pig mask

Snack:

Activity: Apostolic prayers on map and poster

When We Don't Pray
Craft: Pig Mask

Supplies:

- Small Paper Plates (Pink)

- Glue

- Pink Construction Paper

- Craft Sticks

Directions:

Step 1- Take a small Pink Plate.

Step 2- Draw two small circles for the eyes, and cut the circles

for the eyes.

Step 3- For the snout, draw a larger circle with the pink

construction paper.

Step 4- Use the construction paper to make triangles for pig ears.

Step 5- Glue the ears to the plate's top and

the nose to the plate.

Step 6- Glue the Craft stick to the back of the mask to make

a handle.

(For the sake of time, the teacher can cut the ears, eyes,

and noses before class.)

Part II

Apostolic Prayers

List of Apostolic Prayers In This Book

Acts 2:17

2 Thessalonians 3:1

2 Thessalonians 3:5

Ephesians 1:17

Ephesians 1:18

Colossians 1:9-10

Phillipians 1:9

Ephesians 3:18

Colossians 4:3

Romans 15:13

Jeremiah 29:11

Lesson: The Upper Room
Apostolic Prayer Acts 2:17

"Pour Out Your Spirit on your sons and daughters that they may prophesy, see visions, and dream dreams. Show Us your signs and wonders!!"

Lesson Acts 1:1-5, 8-11 (CEB)

Before Jesus ascended to heaven, He instructed His disciples to remain in Jerusalem and wait for the Father's promise. He said,

"This is what you heard from me, 'John baptized with water, but in only a few days, you will be baptized with the Holy Spirit.'"

"You will receive power when the Holy Spirit has come upon you, and you will be my witnesses in Jerusalem, in all Judea and Samaria, and to the ends of the earth." After Jesus said these things, He was lifted above the clouds.

Suddenly, two angels appeared and told the disciples the same Jesus they saw go up would return in the same way. He will return to the same place where He went to heaven, the Mount of Olives.

Acts 2:1-4 When Pentecost came, they were all together in unity. They were in one accord, like-minded, and in one place-the Upper Room.

Suddenly!!!! A sound from heaven rushed into the upper room. A howling wind filled the entire room. They saw what appeared to be flames of fire above the people's heads.

The Upper Room Lesson Continued

Over 3,000 people had gathered from many nations. They were all filled with the Holy Spirit and began to speak in tongues as the Spirit led them.

Explain we are going to pretend this classroom is the upper room. Then, have the children close their eyes and sing "Shekinah Glory" by Cory Asbury & Jay Thomas for a minute or two. Then, wait for the Spirit to fall.

Link to Shekinah Glory: https://www.youtube.com/watch?v=kPml4QdaEls

 Explain this is what the people felt in the 'Upper room.'

Tell them it is incredible, and it is God's heart for them to experience this all the time.

Frequently, daily, not just on Sunday or Wednesday at Church.

  Craft: Flames of fire

 Song time: Sing the Apostolic prayer Acts 2:17

Youtube David Harder videos

https://www.youtube.com/watch?v=QHRE1SMhqig&t=35s

The Upper Room Continued

Review the motions of the Song "Acts 2:17".

Words to Apostolic Prayer Song Acts 2:17

Apostolic Prayer Acts 2:17

"Pour out, pour out your Spirit on your Sons and Daughters

Pour out your Spirit on your Sons and Daughters (repeat a total of four times)

That we may Prophecy! See visions and dream dreams! (repeat 3x)

Show Us Your Signs and Wonders (repeat 2x)

Pour out Your Spirit on Your Sons and Your Daughters (3x)

That we may prophesy, see visions, and dream dreams!! 3x

Show Us your signs and wonders 2x

Motions and tunes can be found on Youtube at David Harder #4

Acts 2:17

Activity: Go to the prayer wall and have them pray Acts 2:17

Family, community, church, school, or world- Their choice.

Then have a few minutes of prayer time.

Apostolic Prayer: Acts 2:17
Upper Room Craft: Tongues Of Fire

Supplies:

- Color Paper to make Headbands

- Flames of Fire is found in the Appendix.

- Glue or Tape

Directions:

Step 1- Before class, cut out flames of fire.

Step 2- Make headbands from strips of paper.

Step 3- Glue flames to the back of headbands.

Step 4- Write "Pour Out Your Spirit" on the front of the

headbands.

Step 5- You can cut up red, orange, and yellow confetti paper and glue it

to the flames.

Lesson: The Great Commission

Apostolic Prayer: 2 Thes. 3:1

"Let The Word of The Lord Run Swiftly and Be Glorified"

Scripture: Matthew 28:16-20, Acts 1:8

Do you remember the story of Jesus' Resurrection? That was when Jesus arose from the grave after dying on the cross. Before He returned to Heaven, working in the power of The Spirit, He instructed His disciples. Jesus revealed Himself to them, demonstrating He was alive! Then, he told them to go to a mountain in Galilee, where He would meet them.

When they saw Jesus, they worshiped Him, but some still doubted it was Jesus. Finally, Jesus told His disciples, "He had received all power and authority in heaven and the earth.

He said, "Therefore, go and make disciples of all nations, baptizing them in the name of the Father, Son, and Holy Spirit, teaching them to obey everything I have commanded you. Look, I will be with you every day until the end of this present age."(Matthew 28:16-20 CEB)

Luke tells us Jesus said we all would be witnesses! Ask, what is a witness? It is someone who tells about an event they saw or experienced. For example, they saw Jesus raised from the dead and witnessed the miracles and healings he performed.

They were to 'GO" tell the people in Jerusalem, Judea, Samaria, and all over the world. He was telling them to take His word "swiftly" so He and His Father may be 'glorified.'

The Great Commission Continued

You are God's witnesses. You can testify or tell others at school, the store, or your family what God has done in your life. His Word can run 'swiftly' through us into the whole world! It can run to the nations and Israel. We tell people Jesus has a plan for their lives.

Craft: Holy Bible

Snack:

Activity: Pray for the world. Have each child pick a nation, city, or region on a map and pray the key Apostolic Prayer, 'Let the Word of The Lord run swiftly.....'
It can be a state within the USA or any nation. Children may also pick their Family members, church, school or community, and neighborhood.

Apostolic Song 1 Thes. 3:1 "Let the Word Of The Lord Run Swiftly and Be Glorified."
Youtube under David Harder #1

https://www.youtube.com/watch?v=06i6QgUfY5Q&t=69s

Apostolic Prayer: 2 Thessalonians 3:1
Lesson: The Great Commission Option One
Craft: Holy Bible

Supplies:

- Copier Paper

- Crayons

Directions:

Step 1- Make copies of 'The Great Commission' page found in the

Appendix.

Step 2- Give the children crayons to color.

Step 3- Have the children color the 'The Great Commission' page.

- Explain God's Word is running swiftly and being glorified

    throughout the world.

Craft: The Great Commission Option Two

Apostolic Prayer: 2 Thessalonians 3:1

"Let the word of the Lord run swiftly and be glorified.

Supplies:

Map of the World found in Appendix.

Crayons

Red Construction Paper

Apostolic Prayer page attached

Glue

Clear paper protectors

Directions:

1. Before class, make little Bibles with the

construction paper, two in. x two in., and write Holy Bible on the front.

2. Make copies of Apostolic Prayer: 2 Thessalonians 3:1 found in Appendix.

3. Give each child a World Map to color.

4. Have the children glue the Apostolic Prayers to

the inside of the Bible.

6. Explain that Prayers are powerful, and they can take their World Map

home and pick a Country to pray for. Then they can tape their Bible

to the Map and pray 2 Thessalonians 3:1 over the country they chose.

Apostolic Prayer 2 Thessalonians 3:5

Lesson: John 3:16 Jesus and Nicodemus

"Now, may the Lord direct your heart into the love of God

and the patience of Christ" (NKJV)

Lesson: The Lord directed Nicodemus to Jesus so Jesus could show him

the love of God. Jesus was patient with Nicodemus.

Nicodemus was one of the Pharisees or religious leaders. These leaders knew the Law and God's word, but it was not in their hearts. There was no relation with God. Nicodemus came to Jesus at night and said, "We know that you came from God because no one does miracles unless God is with them." (John 3:2 CEB)

Jesus answered, "I assure you that unless you are born again, it is impossible to see God's kingdom."

Nicodemus asked, "How is it possible to be born again?"

Jesus answered saying, Nicodemus, you teach the law, and yet you

do not know?"

It is the same as going to church all your life, hearing and reading the word of God, but not knowing Him. There is no relationship with Him.

A lot of people are like that. I (Darlene) was one of those people.

Jesus And Nicodemus Continued

No one but Jesus has come from heaven to earth. We are from the earth and

when we die, we go to be with Jesus in heaven if we have asked Jesus into our hearts.

Jesus must be lifted up so that everyone will believe and have eternal life,

according to John 3:16.

"God so loved the world that He gave His only son so that everyone who

Believes in Him will not perish but have eternal life." (John 3:16 ESV)

Jesus was directing Nicodemus to be saved in his heart and thus have eternal life.

Review salvation (ABC backward). Confess, Believe, and Ask.

Craft:

Activity:

Prayer Time: 2 Thessalonians 3:5

David Harder video #2

https://www.youtube.com/watch?v=06i6QgUfY5Q&t=69s

Lesson: Jesus and Nicodemus

Craft: The Colors of Salvation

Supplies:

Black, Red, White, Purple, Blue, Green,

and Yellow Construction Paper

Copy of Scriptures (Found on the following page)

Scissors

Ribbon

Hole Puncher

Directions:

1. Before class, cut the different colored paper into 6x2 inch size pieces and

give each child one of each color.

2. Cut Scriptures and have the child glue the scriptures to the colored paper.

3. Cut 6-inch-long ribbons.

4. Punch holes at the top of each paper.

5. Thread the colored paper to hold the papers together.

6. While the children are threading papers, tell the children these

scriptures explain salvation to a person who isn't saved.

SCRIPTURE PAGE

Romans 6:23- The wages of sin death.

John 3:16- God so loved the world that he gave his only Son so

    that everyone who believes in him won't perish but

    Will have eternal life.

Romans 10:9- If you confess with your mouth that 'Jesus is Lord' and

believe in your heart that God raised Him from the dead, and you will be saved.

Roman 8:15-16- The Spirit bears witness that we are the children of God.

Matthew 28:19- Therefore, go and make disciples of all the

nations, baptizing them in the name of the Father, the Son, and the Holy Spirit.

Joshua 1:8-9- Recite the Scripture day and night so that you can obey everything

written in the Word.

John 14:1-3- In heaven, there are many rooms God has prepared for us to live in, and

God will come back and take us.

    *All scriptures on this page are taken from Common English Bible

Lesson: Learning The Lord's Ways Part I

Apostolic Prayer: 2 Thes. 3:5

"Now, May the Lord direct your heart into the love of God and into the patience of Christ." (NKJV)

Lesson: One day, I watched my daughter approach her dad. She wanted him to look at something. She became impatient because he didn't look at it right away. She grew angry and stormed off.

As soon as she did that, God showed me that Christians act like that toward Him. We come to the Father, desiring Him to look at our situation immediately!

When God doesn't respond the way we want Him to, we get angry, throw a tantrum and say, "You don't care about us," "You don't love me," or "You love them more than me."

When my daughter acts like that, I want to wait for more, teach her patience, and come back with a better attitude. Often, this is why our prayers go unanswered or there is a delay.

I am reminded of the Children of Israel in the wilderness, with all their complaints. They complained to Moses because they were hungry. They wanted to go back to Egypt. Read Exodus 16 for more.

They threw a tantrum in the desert. They said, "There is no food here. Was it because there were no graves in Egypt that we left?"

Learning The Lord's Ways Part I Continued.

They thought back to the tables in Egypt, where they had meat and bread. They were complaining to God and putting Him to the test.

God decided to test them to see if they would obey Him or follow instructions. The Lord told Moses He would send bread from the sky for six days, and on the 7th day, there would be no bread. So they needed to gather two days worth on the 6th day.

They complained that there was no meat, so He sent quail or birds like a dove. The quail and Manna came for six days. Some people still went out on the 7th day to gather manna but found none.

The Lord asked them, "How long will you refuse to obey My commandments and instructions?"

The Children of Israel ate manna until they came to the edge of Canaan. Despite all their complaining, God still loved them and fed them as a loving Father. Earthly fathers do this when children complain; they still supply our needs.

Craft: Bread from heaven

Apostolic prayer (youtube David Harder) 2 Thes. 3:5

"Now May the Lord direct Your(our) heart into the love of God and into the Patience of God."

https://www.youtube.com/watch?v=06i6QgUfY5Q&t=69s

Prayer Time: Let each child pray for family, friends, church, community, or the nations.

Apostolic Prayer: 2 Thessalonians 3:5

Lesson: Learning the Lord's Way
Craft: Bread from Heaven

Supplies:

- Brown Lunch Bags

- Coriander Seeds

- Crayons

Directions:

1. Give each child a Brown bag.

2. Have the children color the bag.

3. After the children color their bags, have them pretend they are sleeping.

4. While they are sleeping, scatter the seeds on the floor.

5. Then, say, "Wake up and gather your bread from Heaven."

6. Explain that the Manna was similar to Coriander Seed, and the Israelites would grind it and make bread out of the seed.

Apostolic Prayer Ephesians 1:17

Lesson: Revelation of Jesus

Apostolic prayer: Ephesians 1:17

"That The God of Our Lord Jesus Christ May Give To You

The Spirit of Wisdom and Revelation In The Knowledge Of Him."

Lesson Matthew 3:1-17 (CEB)

The Revelation of Jesus begins with John the Baptist, who appeared in the desert of Judea, preaching: "Change your hearts and lives- Here comes the Kingdom of Heaven."

He was (is) the one of whom Isaiah the prophet spoke when he said: "The voice of one shouting in the wilderness, prepare the way for the Lord, Make His path straight." (Matthew 3:3 CEB)

John wore clothes made from the hair of a camel. He had a leather belt and ate locusts and wild honey. John revealed Jesus to the people. John baptized those who changed their hearts and lives.

John said one would come after him that was stronger and mightier than him and that he was not worthy to carry His sandals. Then, he will baptize you with the Holy Spirit and with fire.

Revelation Of Jesus Continued

Jesus came from Galilee to the Jordan River to be baptized by him. John tried to stop Jesus, saying, "I need to be baptized by you, yet you come to me?"

Jesus answered, "Allow Me to be baptized by you now. This is necessary to fulfill all righteousness." So, John agreed.

When Jesus was baptized, Heaven opened as He came out of the water. John saw the Holy Spirit rest on Jesus 'like a dove.'

A voice from heaven declared: "This is My Son whom I dearly love, and I find joy in Him, and I completely delight in Him." (CEB)

Ask what does it mean to delight in someone? It means you find complete satisfaction. Explain happiness is conditional on certain things, but joy is not.

For example, we are happy on our birthday when we receive gifts. But, when it's over, we are not happy. However, we can find joy because we were blessed on our birthday and can enjoy the gifts every day.

God gave us the 'Spirit of Wisdom and Revelation,' the Holy Spirit. He reveals to us that Jesus is God's beloved Son.

Craft: Revelation of Jesus: Baptism of Jesus

Song: learn Apostolic prayer Ephesians 1:17

https://www.youtube.com/watch?v=QHRE1SMhqig&t=38s

(youtube David Harder children's Apostolic prayers #2

Snack:

Activity: Pray over the map and community prayer wall.

REVELATION OF JESUS - CRAFT

Supplies:

White Construction Paper

Crayons or Markers

Directions:

1. Before class, make copies of "Holy Spirit Reveals God's Son."
   Page found in the Appendix.

2. Using their hand, have the children trace their hand
   on the paper. Explain to the children not to
   separate fingers; only separate their thumb from the
   fingers.

3. Draw an eye, a beak, and feet.

4. Write Jesus on the bottom of the paper.

Learning The Lord's Ways Part 2
Apostolic Prayer: Ephesians 1:17

"I pray that the God of our Lord Jesus Christ, the Father of glory, will give you a spirit of wisdom and revelation that makes God known to you." (CEB)

Lesson: 2 Kings 5 (NIV) Learning the Lord's ways are not our ways reminds me of the story of Naaman.

The story begins with Naaman, a general in the army of the King of Aram (Syria). He was a great man with his master and highly regarded since God used him to win a major victory for the king of Aram. He was a brave leader.

But he had one big problem. He had a disease called leprosy. Leprosy is a severe skin condition that can be spread to other people, causing their skin to be scarred. It disfigures people. People with leprosy were required to live away from everyone else, alone or with other lepers.

A young servant girl from Israel told Naaman about a prophet living in Samaria. He could cure Naaman of his leprosy. Naaman sought the king's permission to go to the prophet. The king said yes and sent letters to the king of Israel, along with silver, gold, and fine clothes.

Learning The Lord's Ways Part 2 Continued

At this point, take a letter previously written from an envelope addressed to the king and read it to the class. It can be a simple letter, just something to make the point.

When the king of Israel read the letter, he tore his clothes and said, "Am I God?" "Can I kill something and bring it back?" "Why does he send me someone to be cured of leprosy?" Is he trying to pick a fight with me?

Elisha heard Naaman was coming and told the king to send Naaman to him so he would 'know' there is a prophet in Israel!

When Naaman arrived, he went to Elisha's house and stopped at his door. Elisha sent his messenger to tell Naaman, "Go wash in the Jordan River seven times, and your flesh will be restored, and you will be cleansed."

But, Naaman went away angry, saying, "I thought he would come out and call on the name of God, and wave his hand and cure me. Are not the rivers of Damascus better?"

Naaman's servant told him, " My father, if the prophet told you to do some great thing, then you would have done it. How much more when he tells you to wash and be clean?"

Naaman dipped seven times in the Jordan River, and his flesh was restored and became like that of a young child or baby.

This lesson shows that the Lord's way is the best. Naaman was healed and learned there is no God except the God of Israel.

Learning The Lord's Ways Part 2 Continued

Have you ever wondered why some people do things in certain ways? Or, why do your parents do things differently than everyone else?

As Christians, we are supposed to do things in God's way and not the world's. But we need wisdom and revelation from God the Father through Jesus to help us.

Prayer Time: Ephesians 1:17
https://www.youtube.com/watch?v=QHRE1SMhqig&t=38s Fast Forward to #5
 Snack

Craft: The Naaman Craft

Craft: Naaman Learning The Lord's Ways Part II

Supplies:

The coloring page of Naaman Before/ Naaman After found

in the Appendix.

Crayons or markers

Red Dot stickers

Directions:

1. Before class, make copies of the coloring page

    for each child.

2. Have the children color their paper.

3. Have the children put Red dots on the side of the

    paper that says "Naaman Before."

Jesus Healed With Compassion

Apostolic Prayer: Ephesians 1:17

"That the God of our Lord Jesus Christ would give to you a spirit of wisdom and
   revelation in the knowledge of Him."

Lesson: Jesus was moved with compassion, and as a result, He healed all their diseases.

   Key verses: Matthew 9:35-36 "And Jesus was going about all of the cities and
villages, teaching in their synagogues and proclaiming the gospel of the Kingdom
and healing every kind of sickness."

"And seeing the multitudes, He felt compassion for them because they were distressed
and downcast like sheep without a shepherd."

The Bible teaches Jesus went about doing good. Yet, certain religious leaders
thought what He did was not good. They were supposed to be teachers
that recognized when God was at work. But, sadly, they didn't!

 Furthermore, they accused Jesus of doing good by the hand of the devil. That's
 like doing what your parents tell you, and someone tells you it is from the devil.
Nevertheless, their accusations didn't stop Jesus.

Jesus continued to have compassion for the sick. Ask, "Does anyone know what
compassion is? According to Oxford Languages, compassion is pity and concern for the
sufferings and misfortunes of others.

Jesus Healed With Compassion Continued

For example, you see someone hurting and feel concerned. They cry, and you cry. You feel their emotions and pain with them. You identify with their need, making you want to do something to help.

Jesus went deeper. He looked at the people and saw them as sheep without a shepherd or someone to lead, guide, and help them in every way. The scribes, the Pharisees, and the Sadducees were not leading with the Heart of God the Father.

Jesus' pity, concern, and compassion moved him to act. Sometimes we act in different ways. We may go where they are and do kind things or just pray.

Going to feed the homeless, giving someone a cup of cold water, buying a meal, or just laying your hand on their shoulder and asking, "is everything ok" are ways we can demonstrate compassion. Praying with them is also more powerful than you might think.

In Matthew 14:14, Jesus saw a multitude from a boat. He got out of the boat, went ashore, and 'healed their sickness'. We have to get out of the boat. If Jesus brought the Kingdom of God to the earth, and we believe we are in the Kingdom of God, we can also heal the sick through Jesus.

Pray and ask God to give us compassion for the sick, hurting, lost, or anyone we meet. Pray for their healing, deliverance, or needs to be met. Lord, give us compassion.

Craft: Jesus Healed with Compassion

Snack and Activity

Prayer Time: Ephesians 1:17 https://www.youtube.com/watch?v=QHRE1SMhqig&t=38s
Continue to pray for families, church, community, and the nations, praying for compassion and asking Jesus to heal them and set them free.

Craft: JESUS HEALED WITH COMPASSION

Supplies:

> White Poster Board
>
> Heart Pattern: Found in Appendix
>
> Gold Shiny Pipe Cleaners
>
> Markers
>
> Scissors
>
> Hole Puncher
>
> Bandaids

Directions:

1. Before class, take the heart pattern and trace the pattern on the white poster board for each child.

2. Cut the gold pipe cleaners in half.

3. Write the words "JESUS SAVES" on the heart. (see sample)

4. Give each child two bandaids.

5. Have each child put the bandaids on the heart in the shape of a cross. (show the sample)

6. Have the children decorate their hearts.

OUR NEW BEGINNING: SALVATION

APOSTOLIC PRAYER: Ephesians 1:17

We are going to learn about Salvation through Jesus using the creation story. Genesis 1:1, "In the beginning, God created the heavens and the earth." Did you know, in the beginning, God had a plan for each of us? Yes, even when He created the world, He had a plan for us. Isn't that awesome?

While God was creating the animals, birds, and fish, He was thinking about everyone. I know it is hard to understand. I have a hard time understanding how a very big thought like that. But, He was thinking about me. He was thinking about you, too.

Jeremiah 1:5 reads, "Before I formed you in the womb I knew you, and before you were born I consecrated you; I appointed you to be a prophet to the nations." So, if God knew Jeremiah before he was born, God knew you and me before we were born.

Let's look at Genesis 1:2, "The earth was without form and void, and darkness was over the face of the deep. And the Spirit of God was hovering over the face of the waters." So before we asked Jesus in our hearts, we were spiritually in darkness without Him. God's Spirit was watching over us and wanted us to be with Jesus.

In Genesis 1:3, we read, "And God said, "'Let there be light'" and there was light."God saw it was dark without Jesus, so He sent Jesus to be the Light in our hearts because Jesus is the Light of the world, according to John 8:12. When we ask Jesus in our hearts, our hearts aren't dark anymore because we have Jesus. So, we can be light to people who need Jesus.

Our New Beginning: Salvation Continued

And the way to have Jesus in our hearts and have a new beginning in Christ is to remember the ABCs of Salvation.

1. A- Ask Jesus into your heart.

2. B- Is to believe He is the Son of God.

3. C- Confess our sins. Remember, sin is anything Jesus would NOT do!

Now you are a new creation in Jesus. Jesus is your salvation.

Craft:

Apostolic Prayer time: Ephesians 1:17

https://www.youtube.com/watch?v=QHRE1SMhqig&t=38s

Worship

Pray for salvation, family, community, or nations, etc.

Craft: Our New Beginning: Salvation

Supplies:

        Black Construction Paper

        White Construction Paper

        Scissors

        Glue

        Crayons

Directions:

        Step 1- Cut out one Black Heart and one White Heart.

        Step 2 - Have the children glue both hearts together.

        Step 3 - Have the children write "Without Jesus" with a White crayon.

        Step 4 - Have the children write "With Jesus" with a Red crayon.

        Step 5 - Explain to the children when you don't have Jesus in your heart, it will become black. When when you ask Jesus into your heart, it becomes Clean and white.

Lesson: The Eyes Of Your Understanding

Apostolic Prayer: Ephesians 1:18

"The Eyes of your understanding being enlightened so that you may know the hope of His calling."

Matthew 13:10-16, Isa. 6:9-10, Deut. 29:4 (CEB)

One day, Jesus' disciples came and asked Him, "Why do you use parables when you teach?"

What is a parable? It is a simple story used to illustrate a moral or spiritual lesson told by Jesus in the gospels. It is a story using terms of the earth to describe the kingdom of Heaven!

Consider the parable of the soils found in Matthew 13:3-9

A farmer went out to scatter seeds: As he scattered seeds, some fell on the path, and birds came and ate the seeds. Others fell on rocky ground where there was little or no soil, and thus the seeds sprouted quickly, but the sun scorched them, and they could not take root and dried up quickly.

The other seeds fell on thorny ground. After the seeds sprouted, the thorny plants choked them out and died.

Eyes of Our Understanding Continued

Finally, the remaining seed fell on good soil, sprouted and took root, and grew to bear much fruit. The Holy Spirit says, "If you have ears, then listen to what Jesus is saying."

After He spoke the parable, His disciples asked, "Why do you use parables when you talk to crowds of people.?" Jesus answered, "Because they have not yet received the secrets of the Kingdom of Heaven."

The parables are ways for their eyes to be enlightened and their hearts to understand God's kingdom.

You must be a Christian, or disciple of Jesus, to understand the Kingdom of God. Only the Holy Spirit can reveal it to you. It was prophesied from Isa. 6:9-10 and Deut. 29:4, that some people would not understand.

*The meaning and application of the parable:

On the path, the scattered seeds are the people who hear the word of God and don't understand, and evil comes and snatches it from them.

Rocky ground: They receive the word joyfully and have no root, and it only lasts a little while.

Seed on the thorny ground:

The people who hear the word but the world's worries and false teachings choke out the true word, bearing no fruit.

Eyes of Our Understanding Continued

Seeds on good ground:

The people who hear the word and understand are the ones that bear good fruit.

We pray the "Eyes of our understanding will be enlightened so we may know what the Hope of Your calling is." Then we can bear good fruit.

Craft: Bearing Good Fruit

Snack:

Apostolic prayer: Ephesians 1:18 sing/worship.

https://www.youtube.com/watch?v=2mgxFYcUqKA

Prayer cave: A time of intimacy with the Lord.

Activity: Peep eye, saying the Apostolic Prayer

Craft: Bearing Good Fruit
Ephesians 1:18

Supplies:

    Paper Plates

    Coloring Page

    Crayons

Directions:

1. A coloring page of fruit found in the Appendix.

2. To save time, you can cut Fruit out before class.

3. Fold paper plates in half to form a basket and staple the sides.

4. Color basket

5. Write on the basket-Bearing Good Fruit

6. Have the children put their fruit in the basket.

Invitation To The Wedding

Apostolic Prayer: Ephesians 1:18 "Pray that the eyes of your heart will have enough light to see what is the hope of God's call......." (CEB)

Key Verses: Matthew 9:38: "Pray to the Lord of the Harvest that He will send laborers for the harvest." NIV

Matthew 22:9 "Go therefore to the main roads and invite to the wedding feast as many as you find." ESV

Have you ever been to a wedding? First, you receive an invitation. Maybe you didn't receive an invitation, but your parents did. You probably received an invitation to a birthday party. It's very similar. A wedding is where a man and woman become husband and wife in the eyes of God.

Jesus talked a lot about weddings. That's because there is a wedding coming in heaven. Jesus will marry His bride.

In our lesson, Jesus tells His servants to go out and find people to attend the wedding. It's a parable. Do you remember what a parable is? It is a story using earthly understanding to explain the kingdom of Heaven. Jesus compares a wedding on earth to the marriage in heaven. The servants are us.

Invitation To A Wedding Continued

First, it was for just Israel, but later, people outside Israel got their invitations and could tell others. Jesus is the king who sends out His servants to invite guests to the wedding. The ones He sends out have already come into the Kingdom of God. They are serving Jesus. They have surrendered their lives to Him.

The other people are guests. They don't know Jesus yet. They don't believe in Him, nor do they serve Him.

Which group are you in? Are you inviting people to the wedding and telling others about Jesus? Or are you waiting for your invitation? Maybe you have your invitation but have not said yes to Jesus.

Pray with the children about asking Jesus into their hearts and being born into the kingdom of God.

You will not want to miss the wedding in heaven. But, if you have not surrendered and made Jesus the Lord and Savior of your life, now is the time.

1) Pray for all to receive Jesus. Say yes to His invitation.

2) Pray for all to have hearts to go and give out invitations to the wedding for others to become followers of Jesus.

3) Pray for lost people everywhere to receive Jesus.

Craft: Invitation To A Wedding

Apostolic Prayer: Ephesians 1:18 https://www.youtube.com/watch?v=2mgxFYcUqK

Craft: INVITATION TO A WEDDING

Supplies:

    Paper plates

    Markers

    Red Hearts (see Example)

    Glue

Directions:

1. Before class, cut red hearts out and write a Nation on each heart. For example-USA, Kenya, Ukraine, etc.

2. Put the hearts in a paper sack and write on the outside: GIFTS FOR THE MARRIAGE SUPPER OF THE LAMB (Option you can decorate the sack)

3. Write on each Paper plate: Marriage Supper of the Lamb

4. Give each child a paper plate and have them decorate the plate.

5. After they decorate their plate, have them pick a red heart

6. Tell the child to take the plate home and pray for that nation to come to Christ.

Lesson: Gideon: Mighty Man of God Part I

Apostolic Prayer: Colossians 1:10 "That you may have a walk worthy of the Lord and to be strengthened with all might."

Scripture for Lesson: Judges chapters 6-7

Today, we will be studying Gideon. When he was mashing grapes for juice, an angel from God appeared to him and said, "The Lord is with you, mighty warrior!" The Lord told Gideon, "You have strength, go and rescue (deliver) Israel from the power of Midian. Am I not the one sending you?"

Gideon was afraid and asked God to confirm what He was asking Gideon to do. So he put out the 'fleece' on the threshing floor.

A threshing floor is a hard surface where farmers separate the grain from the husk, like wheat. However, it can be used as Gideon used to trample grapes.

Fleece is the skin and wool of a sheep in one piece. It's like a coat.

Gideon told the Lord if there was dew on the fleece, but the ground was dry, he would know He was sending him to rescue Israel. That's what happened to Gideon. He squeezed the fleece, and the dew filled up a bowl.

Gideon wasn't satisfied. He asked God not to be angry. Instead, he asked for another sign. He asked for the fleece to be dry and the ground to be wet the next morning. So that is what God did.

Ask: Have you ever asked for something but were unsure what to ask? Maybe you doubted as Gideon did!

Gideon: Mighty Man Of God Part 1 Continued

We often feel like we've heard a word from God, but we want confirmation. Gideon was no different. He sought confirmation that God was sending him to defeat the Midianites since they were fierce and outnumbered the Israelites. They oppressed Israel, so Gideon wanted to be sure God was sending him. He knew if God sent him, God would be the one fighting.

You can be confident if God calls you or tells you to do something. He will guide you every step of the way. It is easy to say we believe what God says, but when He tells us to do something big, we still want proof it is from God, just like Gideon.

Craft: Dry fleece on wet ground

Apostolic prayer: Colossians 1:10 "Walk worthy of the Lord and be strengthened with all might."

David Harder's Youtube video for Colossians 1:10

https://youtu.be/06i6QgUfY5Q

Prayer time: Use the verse to pray for family, church, community, and the nations to "walk worthy of the Lord."

Apostolic Prayer
Colossians 1:10-11

I wanna walk, walk, walk (3x)

Worthy of the Lord

I wanna walk, walk, walk, (3x)

Worthy of the Lord

And Be strengthened with all might (huh) (3x)

Walk worthy of the Lord.

And be strengthened with all might (huh) (3x)

Walk worthy of the Lord.

Youtube video Apostolic prayers songs #-3 David Harder
https://youtu.be/06i6QgUfY5Q

Apostolic Prayer: Colossians 1:19-1

"That you may walk worthy of the Lord, fully pleasing Him, being fruitful in

every good work and increasing in the knowledge of God; being strengthened

with all might according to His glorious power, for all patience with longsuffering

and joy." (NKJV)

Gideon Mighty Man of God Part I

Craft 1: Dry Fleece on Wet Ground

Supplies:

       Green Construction Paper

       Glue

       Faux Fleece

       Water

Directions:

1. Cut the green paper in half

2. Cut two faux fleece, smaller than the green paper

3. Glue the fleece on the green paper

4. Add a drop of water to one of the fleece

5. Explain to the children how Gideon prayed

    for the fleece to be wet and dry

Lesson: Gideon Mighty Man of God Part II

Gideon Prepares For Battle.

The Scripture for the lesson is in Judges chapters 6-7

As Gideon prepared to go to battle, the Lord said, "You have too many men." Yes, if He handed the Midianites over to Gideon and his men like that, they would take credit for what God did.

God said to tell the men anyone who was afraid or unsteady could go home. So, 22,000 men left and returned home.

But God said, "There are still too many men." So He instructed Gideon to take them down to the water, and He would tell him who could go with him.

When Gideon and the men arrived at the water, the Lord said to set aside those who lap the water with their tongues like a dog from those who bend down.

The number of men who lapped, putting their hands to their mouths, was 300. The rest bent down on their knees to drink the water with their hands to their mouths.

That night, the Lord told Gideon, "Get up and 'attack.'"

He said, "I have handed the Midianites over to you. But, if you are afraid, go down to the camp with a servant, and you will hear what they are saying. May you have the courage to fight." So He went to the enemy's camp.

As Gideon arrived, he heard a man saying I had a dream, and in it, a loaf of barley bread was rolling into the Midianite camp. It hit a tent, and the tent collapsed and fell flat.

The man said God had handed Midian over to Gideon.

Gideon: Mighty Man Of God Part II Continued

Gideon heard that and said, "Get up; the Lord has handed Midian over to us."

Gideon divided the 300 into three units and equipped every man with a shofar and an empty jar with a torch inside.

Then, Gideon told them to do what he did. "When I blow the shofar, each man will blow his shofar and surround the camp."

Shout! Shout "For the Lord and Gideon!"

Then they smashed the jars holding the torches.

Suddenly, the Lord turned the Midianites to fight each other. Then the whole Midianite camp fled.

So God defeated the Midianites by the hand of Gideon.

Craft: shofars and jars

Apostolic prayer: Colossians 1:10 "walk worthy of the Lord and be strengthened with all might."

David Harder's Youtube video for Colossians 1:10

https://youtu.be/06i6QgUfY5Q

Prayer time: Continue praying for families, leaders, teachers, and the nations to walk worthy of The Lord!

Craft: Gideon: Mighty Man Of God Part II

Gideon Prepares For Battle

Craft 2- Shofar And The Jars For Torches

Supplies:

Shofar: White card stock

A pattern of a shofar, found in Appendix

String

Hole Puncher

Crayons

Tape

Directions For The Shofar:

1. Before class, trace the shofar on the white card stock

2. To save time, cut out the shofar pattern

3. Have children color the shofar

4. Have children tape the shofars together

5. Punch holes to put a string through so they can wear them around their necks

Apostolic Prayer Philippians 1:9

Lesson: The Word (Bible) And The Spirit
Key Verse: John 1:1-5

Apostolic Prayer: Philippians 1:9 "That your love may abound still more

and more, in   all knowledge and discernment."

Lesson- To have knowledge and discernment of God's love. This comes through

prayer, reading, and understanding the Word of God, the Bible.

John 1:1-5 (CEB) The story of the Word-- Jesus is the Word

"In the beginning was the word, and the word with God, and the Word was God. The Word was

with God in the beginning. Everything came into being through the Word, and without the Word,

nothing came into being. What came into being through the Word was life, and the light was life

for all people. The light shines in the darkness, and the darkness doesn't extinguish the light."

Through the Bible, we know about Jesus. We discover who He is, what He has done and will

do. The Bible is God's Word and teaches us Jesus is the light of the world.

We receive knowledge of God's love through Jesus by reading His word. Men wrote the

word of God under the direction of the Holy Spirit. So, what we are reading came from

The Word And The Spirit Continued

God's throne through His Spirit to us. Jesus is the fullness of God revealed. When we see Jesus, we see God the Father.

God wants His love to abound in us. What does abound mean? Abound is derived from the word abundance, which means more than enough, or overflowing. So God's desire is for His love to be abundant and overflow. That comes by the revelation of Jesus through His Word.

Think about the Grinch. You know, the mean green guy that 'stole Christmas.' But, he found love, and what happened? His heart grew bigger.

When we ask Jesus into our hearts, our hearts are expanded like the grinches. We have room to receive more of God's love, and we can pour out that love.

We grow to love the Word of God, the Bible.

Craft: Jesus loves me hearts!

Activity:

Apostolic prayer: Philippians 1:9

Pray for the community, families, church, state, neighborhood, the nations, and Israel to abound more and more in God's love.

There is no video for this prayer, but the words and motions are listed below:

Philippians 1:9 Words and Motions

Sing while hopping or jumping around in a straight line: May your love abound

Still more, and more and more and more, and still more, then pause and say

In all knowledge (hold for a few seconds) and understanding.

Craft: The Word and The Spirit

Supplies:

"Jesus Loves Me" - Heart Paper, found in Appendix.

Coloring Pencils

Directions:

1. Before class, make copies of "Jesus Loves Me."

    Heart paper.

2. Have the children draw a picture of themselves inside

the heart.

3. Have the children color the picture of themselves.

Adam and Eve: Consequences of Sin

Apostolic Prayer: Phil. 1:9 "I pray that your love may abound still more and more in knowledge and all discernment. (NKJV)

Key Scripture Genesis 2:15-17, Genesis 3.

What is sin? Anything that Jesus wouldn't do is a good definition of sin. Would Jesus tell a lie? No! Would Jesus steal? No! Would Jesus disobey His parents? No,

We need to be like Jesus and do our best not to sin. It is hard because we are human, and so many things persuade us to do the wrong thing. Obeying God's commands is not an option. That's why they are commands. Jesus is always there to help us and to always do right if we ask.

Our lesson begins with the story of Adam and Eve and the first consequences of sin. God created Adam and Eve and placed them in a beautiful garden called 'Eden.' He told them to name the animals and rule over everything.

There were plenty of fantastic things, such as the most delicious food you could ever imagine. All kinds of trees and plants, including the most beautiful flowers, were in the garden. God placed them in charge of this lush paradise. Their job was to take care of this garden. They were also to love, obey and worship the Lord God.

The garden, called 'Eden,' contained a special tree. "What was so special about this tree?" It was called the 'Tree of the Knowledge of Good and Evil.' The Lord had specifically told them they could eat fruit from any tree except this one. That was

Adam And Eve: Consequences of Sin Continued

the only thing He told them not to do. God told them if they ate its fruit,

they would surely die.

Imagine your grandmother has a whole orchard of fruit and nut trees. She says you can

eat from the peach, pear, apple, pecan, walnut, and cherry trees. But in the middle is a fig bush. It

is so big, and the fruit is so juicy, but you are not allowed to touch it, or you will die.

One day the serpent, or snake, came and talked with Eve. Now this serpent was different.

He sweet-talked Eve and said, "Did you actually hear God tell you not to eat of this tree?

Perhaps that is just something your husband Adam told you. Don't you think figs are good for

you? They make great preserves and jellies."

But, Eve told the old serpent that they could eat of any tree in the garden except for one, 'The

tree of the Knowledge of Good and Evil.' She told the serpent they would die just by touching it.

What God said was, 'don't eat it.'

The snake lied to Eve, just like every wrong thought you get is a lie from Satan. What if

he told you to eat from the fig tree, even though grandma said not to? The snake told Eve the

day she and Adam ate from that tree, they would be just like God, knowing good and evil.

Eve took a bite of the fruit and gave some to Adam. I am sure that it was delicious fruit.

But then something happened. They saw everything differently and noticed they needed clothes.

So Adam and Eve told God they were naked, which is how they confessed to disobeying Him.

Adam And Eve: Consequences of Sin Continued

We know sin is wrong. Sin is breaking God's commandments. Just like breaking any rule, there is a punishment. What was Adam and Eve's punishment?

They had to leave the garden and would have to work harder than before to get food. Adam and Eve lost their paradise.

Let us pretend we are driving a car. There is a gas pedal and a brake pedal. The gas pedal makes it go, while the brake makes it stop.

One day your mom makes some cookies and places them in a cookie jar. She tells you not to eat them until after supper. Those cookies smell delicious and look so good, and in your head, you hear a voice saying, "Go ahead; she will never know. She won't even miss it!" Remember Adam and Eve!

You have to put the brakes on and silence that voice. You tell it that is not the point. Mom said not to eat one, not even a bite. So, I will not eat the cookie. I don't want to receive punishment such as no cookies for a week or no new toys or special treats.

Turn the other way and press the gas pedal into the love of God. He loves us so much sometimes He will allow a jar of cookies to be placed before us that we can't have. He loves us and wants us to obey because we love Him.

Apostolic prayer: Philippians 1:9

Craft: Coloring Page

Activity:

Prayer Time: Pray for the community, church, families, the United States, nations, cities, or regions as led. Pray for God's love to abound in all knowledge and understanding.

Craft: ADAM AND EVE: CONSEQUENCES OF SIN

Supplies:

      1. The coloring page of a Tree labeled 'Do Not Eat The Fruit' is

found in Appendix

      2. Crayons

      3. Glue

Directions:

      1-Before class, make copies for each child of the Tree

      2-Have the children color the Tree and remind them of

      God's command to eat only of the "Good Tree."

      3-Explain how Satan tempted Eve to eat the forbidden fruit

      and how they forgot about the goodness of God.

*Explain God loves us so much that He supplies good things so we will not want to eat the Forbidden fruits of life. This is because we love God so much, and we desire to obey Him.

Lesson: Phillip and The Ethiopian Eunuch

Apostolic Prayer: Ephesians 3:19

"Let us comprehend with all of the saints the love that surpasses knowledge that we may be filled with the fullness of God."

Lesson found in Acts 8: 26-40 (CEB)

A man named Philip was one of the early servants called 'deacons' in the church at Jerusalem. One day an angel appeared to Philip and told him to take the road from Jerusalem to Gaza. Have you ever needed directions on which way to go? Maybe you weren't going anywhere, and someone said to go this way or that way. Philip obeyed the angel and took the road to Gaza.

A man from Ethiopia was on the same road going home from Jerusalem. He was one of the queen's servants and was in charge of her treasury. So, he was an important man in Ethiopia.

He had been to Jerusalem to worship at the temple. He was reading Isaiah 53:7-8 when the Holy Spirit told Philip to go to his chariot. So, Philip walked alongside the chariot and heard him reading. He asked him if he understood what he was reading.

He answered, "I do not understand what I am reading. I need someone to teach me." So that is what we are trying to teach you here so that you understand.

These are the words that the eunuch read: "Like a sheep, He was led to the slaughter, and like a lamb, before its shearer is silent, so he didn't open His mouth. In His humiliation, justice was taken away from Him. Who can tell the story of His descendants because His life was taken from the earth?"

Phillip and The Ethiopian Eunuch Continued

The Ethiopian asked, "Who is he speaking of?" Philip explained He was talking about Jesus. Then, the Ethiopian suddenly exclaimed, "Look, there is much water. What is preventing me from being baptized?"

They went down to the water, and Philip baptized him there.

When they came up from the water, the Holy Spirit suddenly took Philip away. The man from Ethiopia never saw him again. So the Ethiopian was filled with God's fullness and love. He became joyful and began to sing and rejoice.

Now is a good time if you haven't experienced the fullness of God's love. First, talk to your parents and leaders. Then, after you believe and receive Jesus, do like Philip and be baptized, or immersed underwater, showing the world you have received God's complete love and are following Jesus as His disciple.

Apostolic prayer: Ephesians 3:19

"Let us comprehend with all of the saints the love that surpasses knowledge that we may be filled with the fullness of God."

Craft: Jesus is the lamb. Cross and lamb.

Snack/Activity

Prayer time. Have the children pray this verse over family, church, community, nations, leaders, etc., as led.

Worship and private prayer (cave) time.

Craft: Phillip and The Ethiopian Eunuch

Supplies:

"Jesus Is The Lamb" - Paper, found in the Appendix.

Glue sticks or Glue

Cotton Balls

Directions:

1. Before class, make copies of "Jesus Is The Lamb" for each child.

2. Give each child a Glue Stick. (Optional-You can put some in a small bowl and have the children dip their cotton balls in the glue.

3. Have the children glue the cotton balls to the Lamb.

Apostolic Prayer: Colossians 4:3

Lesson: Open Doors In Effective Ministry

Colossians 4:3 "Pray That God may open to us a door for the word so that we may speak forth the mystery of Christ, for which I also am imprisoned."

Lesson Scripture: Acts 14:27

"When they arrived and gathered the church together, they declared all God had done with them and how he had opened a door of faith to the Gentiles."

Before Jesus went back to be with the Father in Heaven, He told his disciples to go and tell people everywhere the good news of the Kingdom of God.

Later, Jesus called Paul, a Jew, to spread the good news to the Gentiles (nations). Previously, Jews only went to other Jews. But, God loves all nations and wants them to hear the Good News of His Kingdom.

Paul wrote to the people in Colossae, a city in modern Turkey, to pray for a 'door' or opportunity to share the good news to open.

We are to share with everyone Jesus that heals, delivers, saves, and provides. We must tell all Jesus has done. That's the Good News of the Kingdom of Heaven, which has now come to the earth through Him.

But not everyone will listen or understand. We meet all kinds of people, and many do not want to hear the good news of the Kingdom of God.

Open Doors In Effective Ministry Continued

We must pray that people have hearts and minds to be 'open' to hearing the good news daily. Explain how we don't always want to listen to what our parents and teachers tell us. Sometimes things hinder us from sharing the Good News with others.

In Acts 14, Paul and Barnabas went to a place called Antioch. God had opened a 'door' of faith to the Gentiles, or non-Jews, to hear and receive the Good News!
ASK: What is a door of faith?
It is an opportunity to share the good news, and we believe it will be received by faith.

Here, we discussed the homeless ministry and an open door of faith. We feed the homeless and pray for an open door when they arrive. We want them to listen and receive the gospel. *Use your own stories as led.*

We need an opening to share the Good News when we are around people who do not know God or Jesus. We must ask God to open a 'door' for us to speak about Jesus and for their hearts to receive.

Craft: Open Doors

Snack/Activity:

"Pray for open doors to speak the good news of the kingdom of heaven."
Have children pray Col. 4:3 over themselves, their family, church, the USA, other nations Israel, etc., and the homeless.

Craft: Open Doors

Supplies:

White Construction Paper

Brown Construction Paper

Crayons

Stapler

Stickers

Directions -

1. Give each child a piece of White and Brown Construction paper each..

2. On the Brown Construction paper, draw and have the children decorate their door with stickers and crayons.

3. On the White Construction paper, write "SHARE THE GOOD NEWS" and have each child write the name of the country they want to pray for. (EX. - Kenya)

4. Help the children staple the door to the white construction paper.

Abounding In Hope

Apostolic Prayer: Romans 15:13 "May the God of hope fill you with all joy and peace in faith so that you overflow with hope by the power of the Holy Spirit." (CEB)

Lesson: Key Verse Proverbs 13:12

"Hope deferred makes a heart sick, but a desire fulfilled is a tree of life. (ESV)

What is hope? It is a feeling or desire for something to happen. It is derived from something we believe we can have, or as children, our parents will provide for us.

I'm talking about something more than a toy or Christmas present. It could be a trip to a place like Disney! Abraham and Sarah had to wait for the son of promise, Isaac. But in their waiting, their heart grew tired of waiting, so they decided to help God.

A child named Ishmael was born to Sarah's maid by Abraham. Later, Sarah got angry, and problems arose. Finally, Sarah made Hagar leave with her child.

A woman named Hannah prayed for a son. Her husband had children from another wife. Explain that men sometimes had more than one wife in those days, but it was not part of God's plan. So Hannah cried for a child. After that, she went to the Tabernacle frequently and prayed. Once, she prayed so hard the priest thought she was drunk.

But God heard her prayer and gave her a son, Samuel, just as God promised Sarah and Abraham. Isaac was born to Sarah when she was a 90-year-old lady.
Ask, what if your grandmother had to wait to be 90 to have your mom or dad?

Abounding Hope Continued

There are many other examples of people who combined waiting with hoping. They believed all of God's promises would come to pass.

When we are hoping for something, we often grow tired, and soon we no longer want it. We quit asking. People do that with prayer. But, instead of growing tired and weary, we should 'hope' with joy!

Yes, we ask the God of Hope, our heavenly Father, to fill us with Joy and Peace in believing. God wants us to overflow with Hope. Hannah is a perfect example of someone abounding with hope.

Hannah did not lose hope. Sarah deferred hope. She had no peace and joy, but Hannah continued with joy and peace.

The Bible is full of stories of people that had to wait and hope. Many lost hope, while others like Moses, Daniel, David, and Joseph continued to 'abound' in hope joyfully.

Prayer: ask God to fill us with joy and peace in believing and abounding in hope.

Craft
Hannah and Samuel- Samuel's coat

Pray Romans 15:13

Worship and prayer cave time: Thank God for all the times He has fulfilled

His promise to provide, etc.

Craft: The God Of Hope
'Samuel's Coat'

Supplies -

A Coloring page of "Samuel's Coat" found in the Appendix.

Crayons or Markers

Stickers

Directions -

1. Before class, make copies of "Samuel's Coat" coloring page for each child.

2. Have children decorate Samuel's coat, with crayons, markers, and stickers.

ISAAC'S WELLS: MAKING PEACE
WITH YOUR ENEMY

Genesis 26:12-32

Apostolic Prayer: Romans 15:13 "May the God of hope fill you with

all joy and peace in faith so that you overflow with hope by the

power of the Holy Spirit."

God blessed Isaac, Abraham's son, who became a wealthy man. He had livestock, such

as sheep and cattle, and servants. However, his enemies grew jealous because of his prosperity

and decided to fill his wells with dirt.

As a result, a ruler named Abimelech told him to leave. The wells Abraham dug were

redug by Isaac after he moved. The first well he dug was called Esek, which meant to quarrel.

While Isaac's shepherds were digging the well, his enemy Gerzar claimed it as his well, so Isaac

left.

Can you guess what happened next? Yes, Isaac dug another well, and his enemy got mad and

argued about that well. So, he named the well Sitnah, meaning an accusation, because his enemy

accused them of taking their well.

I know you can tell what happened next. Sure, he had to dig another well! If this were me, I

would be getting angry. The Bible doesn't say if he got angry. However, Isaac dug another well

which was his third well.

Isaac's Wells: Continued

What do you think happened next? No, the enemy finally left him alone. PRAISE GOD. Isaac named this well Rehoboth meaning open spaces. He had open spaces where there was peace.

Later, Isaac took a trip to Beersheba, and the Lord appeared to him and said, "I AM the God of your father, Abraham. Don't be afraid because I am with you. I will bless you, and I will give you many children for my servant Abraham's sake."

Isaac built an altar, and his servant dug another well. Then, Abimelech came to see him. Isaac is wondering what now? He said to Abimelech, "You resented me and told me to move." Abimelech wasn't angry and came to make peace because He knew God was with Isaac. Finally, Issac prepared a banquet, and they went their separate ways.

Finally, his servant came running and shouted, "WE FOUND WATER!" Isaac called this well Shibah, meaning to give an oath or seven. So, Isaac gave his word and made peace with his enemies.

Even when your enemy is after you, Jesus said to love them. In Luke 6:35-36, "But love your enemies, do good to them, and lend to them without expecting to get anything back."

Craft: Isaac's wells

Apostolic Prayer time:

Snack/Activity:

Prayer cave:

Craft: Isaac's Wells

Supplies:

    *Coloring page of "Isaac's Well," found in the Appendix.

    *Crayons or Markers

Directions:

    1. Before class, make copies of "Isaac's Well" for each child.

    2. Have children color "Isaac's Well" with crayons or markers.

You Are Special: God Knows Your Plans

Apostolic Prayer and Key Verse: Jeremiah 29:11

"For I know the plans that I think towards you, says the Lord, thoughts of peace and not of evil, and to give you a future and a hope." (KJV)

Did you know before the world's creation, The King of the Universe had every one of you in His thoughts? So today, we pray you will receive God's plans and thoughts for each of you.

God's hope is in you. God's future is in you. His destiny is in you. You are on God's mind and heart. He desires for you to be and have all he has for you.

We need to pray for God's will and not our own. We need the Holy Spirit to lead and guide us in the way that we need to go. The Holy Spirit is our guide here on the earth until Jesus comes back.

"Before I formed you in the womb, I knew you; before you were born, I set you apart. I appointed you to be a prophet to the nations." Jer. 1:5 (NIV)

Wow!! Before we were born, our life began to take shape. What God planned for me and you is incredible! Our life is full of what God spoke when He spoke each of us into being. There is no going back.

You Are Special: God Knows Your Plans Continued

We need to stop and thank God for thinking about us and thank Him for our lives. One way we can show our appreciation for Him making us special is to obey Him and His word. We need to obey Him and always ask for His help.

Choosing God is a lifetime commitment. It is our destiny to live for God. When we ask Jesus into our hearts, we make Him King and Lord of our lives, we surrender everything to Him. He owns everything, so he guides our lives through the Holy Spirit.

When He becomes Lord of our lives, joy and gladness will follow us all the days of our lives. This makes all the difference.

We pray for God to be the Lord of our lives.

Craft: You are special faces

Activity:

Prayer time

*This lesson is adapted from "God Knows The Plans", by Sharon Mullins for Mountain Movers Prayer Group, March 2020.

Craft: You Are Special: God's Plans For Your Life

Supplies:

        White Paper Plates

        Crayons or Markers

        Yarn for hair (optional)

        Glue

Directions:

1. Hand each child a paper plate.

2. Pass out crayons or markers.

3. (Optional) You can pre-cut yarn for hair for the glue to the plate.

What's Next?

Congratulations on completing the first book/course in teaching children about prayer and

hearing the voice of God. But this is only the beginning. At least four more books will soon

focus on prayer, worship, and other areas of discipling the next generation.

What's coming? Book II follows, which will take the Sunday school lessons you and I grew up

with and transform them to open up God's heart for the nations and how we can pray for them.

Children will learn how the nations were formed and scattered at Babel and

how God developed Israel as His unique treasure with the goal of bringing back the

nations. That is accomplished through Jesus, and we understand why we are called

to disciple the nations.

Subsequent manuals will focus on the Beatitudes and Jesus' teachings on living the life He calls

us to live. There will be lessons on the Armor of God as well. Then we will study worship

and some examples from the Old and New Testaments. Later we will teach about the

Tabernacle of Moses, the furniture, the priests, the sacrifices, and how Jesus fulfilled all of these.

Finally, we will have studies on Who is God? Who is Jesus? And Who is the Holy Spirit?

We look forward to sharing these with you in the future and partnering with you on your journey.

Blessings, Joseph and Darlene Floyd

Appendix:
Attachments To Crafts and
Coloring Pages

The following pages contain attachments and coloring pages for the crafts in some of the lessons. The craft instructions follow each lesson, and a supply list is included. For the pages that have a statement *found in the Appendix, that paper can be found on the following pages. They are in order as to their corresponding order with the lessons. Not every lesson will have an attachment, however.

Enjoy these lessons, and remember that crafts and coloring pages are provided to help reinforce the material. It enables the students to retain the information learned and provides a visible, tangible demonstration of what they learned to share with friends and family.

We pray the Lord's Blessings to be upon you as you join Jesus in the journey of teaching the next generation to pray, worship and follow Jesus as disciples.

Our Father in heaven,
hallowed be your name.

Your Kingdom Come, Your will be done,
on earth as it is in heaven.

Give us this day, our daily bread.

Forgive us our debts, as we also
have forgiven our debtors.

And lead us not into temptation,
but deliver us from evil.

For Yours is the Kingdom, and
the power and the glory forever, amen.

Matthew 6:9-13 (NIV)

Confidence In Prayer

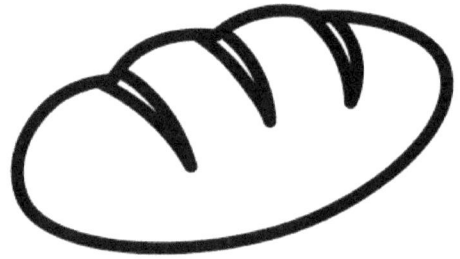

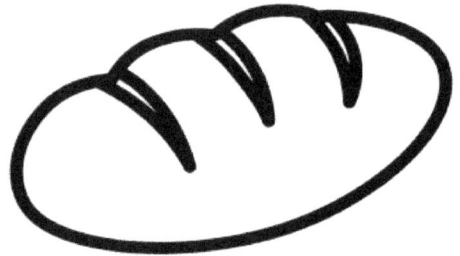

Upper Room

The Great Commiission

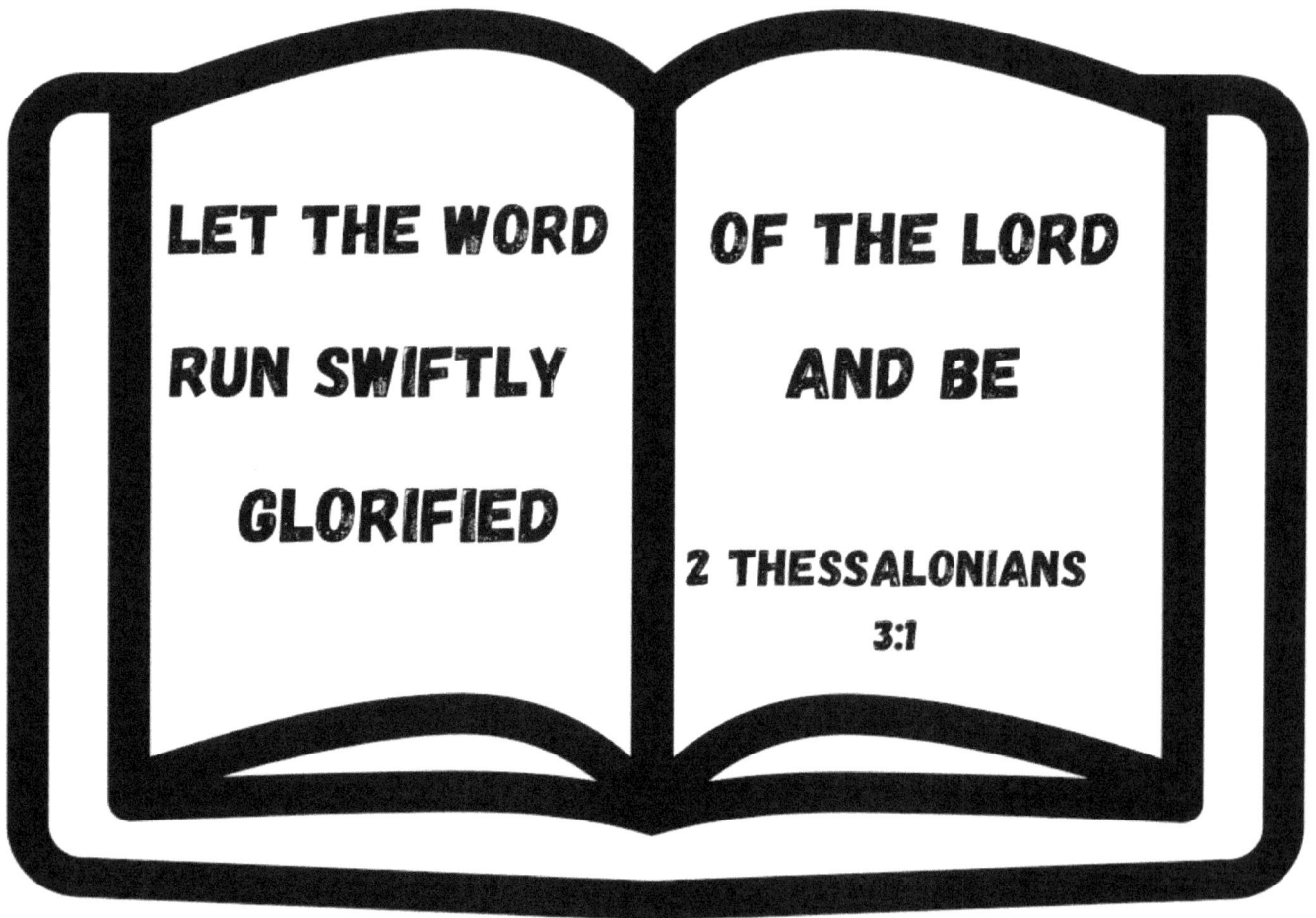

LET THE WORD RUN SWIFTLY GLORIFIED

OF THE LORD AND BE

2 THESSALONIANS 3:1

Great Commission Craft#2

Let the word of the Lord
run quickly and be glorified.
2 Thessalonians 3:1

Let the word of the Lord
run quickly and be glorified.
2 Thessalonians 3:1

Let the word of the Lord
run quickly and be glorified.
2 Thessalonians 3:1

Let the word of the Lord
run quickly and be glorified.
2 Thessalonians 3:1

Let the word of the Lord
run quickly and be glorified.
2 Thessalonians 3:1

Let the word of the Lord
run quickly and be glorified.
2 Thessalonians 3:1

Let the word of the Lord
run quickly and be glorified.
2 Thessalonians 3:1

Let the word of the Lord
run quickly and be glorified.
2 Thessalonians 3:1

Let the word of the Lord
run quickly and be glorified.
2 Thessalonians 3:1

Let the word of the Lord
run quickly and be glorified.
2 Thessalonians 3:1

Let the word of the Lord
run quickly and be glorified.
2 Thessalonians 3:1

Let the word of the Lord
run quickly and be glorified.
2 Thessalonians 3:1

Let the word of the Lord
run quickly and be glorified.
2 Thessalonians 3:1

Let the word of the Lord
run quickly and be glorified.
2 Thessalonians 3:1

Let the word of the Lord
run quickly and be glorified.
2 Thessalonians 3:1

Let the word of the Lord
run quickly and be glorified.
2 Thessalonians 3:1

Let the word of the Lord
run quickly and be glorified.
2 Thessalonians 3:1

Let the word of the Lord
run quickly and be glorified.
2 Thessalonians 3:1

Let the word of the Lord
run quickly and be glorified.
2 Thessalonians 3:1

Let the word of the Lord
run quickly and be glorified.
2 Thessalonians 3:1

Let the word of the Lord
run quickly and be glorified.
2 Thessalonians 3:1

Let the word of the Lord
run quickly and be glorified.
2 Thessalonians 3:1

Let the word of the Lord
run quickly and be glorified.
2 Thessalonians 3:1

Let the word of the Lord
run quickly and be glorified.
2 Thessalonians 3:1

Let the word of the Lord
run quickly and be glorified.
2 Thessalonians 3:1

Let the word of the Lord
run quickly and be glorified.
2 Thessalonians 3:1

Let the word of the Lord
run quickly and be glorified.
2 Thessalonians 3:1

Holy Spirit Reveals
God's Son- Jesus

Naaman- Before

Naaman- After

Jesus Healed With Compassion

Bearing Good Fruit

Gideon's Shofar

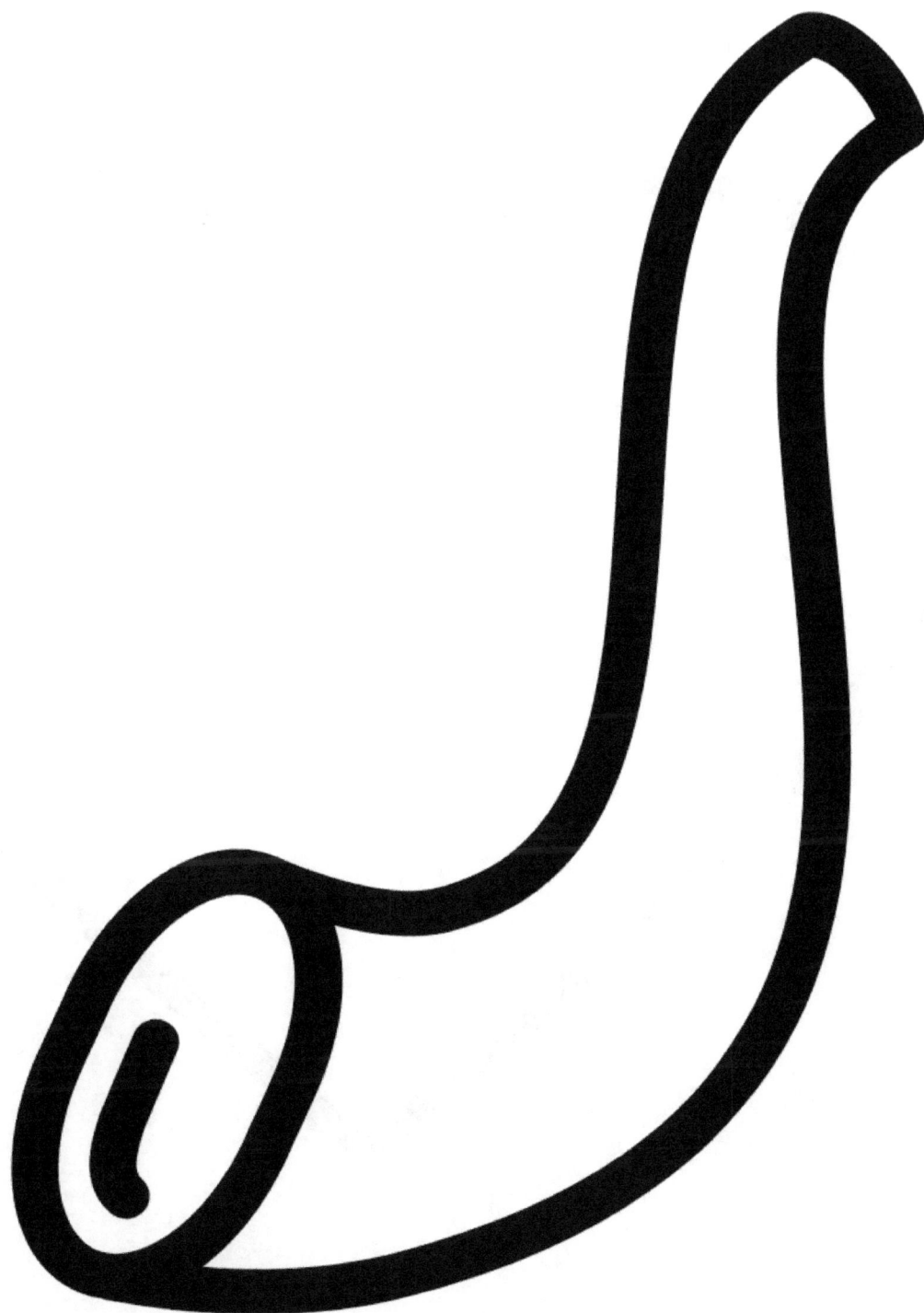

Jesus Loves Me

Forbidden Fruit

Jesus Is The Lamb

Isaiah 53:7-8

Go and Share
The Good News

Pray For an Open door To Share The Good News

Samuel's Coat

Isaac's Wells